More Family Devotions Bas
Carols

Christ-Centered Advent
Volume 2

Hal & Melanie Young

GREAT WATERS PRESS
MAKING BIBLICAL FAMILY LIFE PRACTICAL

Contents

Before You Begin

For many years, we've taught our children the hymns of the faith through what we call the Hymn of the Week. Each day we sing all the verses of the song we're learning and explain one of the verses. By the end of the week, even the young children have learned to sing the hymn and understand it. We can sing for hours in the van without a hymnbook – such a blessing!

This has been particularly precious to us during the Christmas season. Christmas hymns or carols are so full of rich theology that it's a shame to just sing the first verse, which is usually the introduction, and never even consider the rest.

Christians have been celebrating the birth of Christ in song since the 3rd or 4th century. *O Come, O Come Emmanuel* was written twelve hundred years ago! The tradition of caroling, walking from house to house singing Christmas carols, dates back to at least the 13th century.

In this Christmas devotional, we use that ancient tradition and the dear hymns of the Advent season, the time when we anticipate celebrating the Incarnation, when the Word was made flesh, and the birth of Christ, to point our children to the gospel and encourage us all to worship.

Come and join us.

Choose a time when you can all gather for a few minutes. We like to open in prayer. Don't make it too complicated, just ask the Lord to help you all to understand what is being taught and to teach you to love and trust Him.

Sing the entire carol, all the verses, every weekday. We've provided four weeks of devotions with five lessons per week.

After you sing, read the explanation of the verse for that day. Don't worry if it seems over your children's heads. We've been shocked by how much kids can grasp if you give them a chance. Answer any questions and talk about what it means for your lives. Close in prayer, praying about any requests you have. It should take about 15 minutes a day. If you keep it short and doable, you won't have as much trouble doing it consistently!

Enjoy!

The Christmas Carols

For the next few weeks, we are going to be using Christmas carols as the basis for our devotions! Let's read what the Bible says about singing:

Look carefully then how you walk, not as unwise but as wise, making the best use of the time, because the days are evil. Therefore do not be foolish, but understand what the will of the Lord is. And do not get drunk with wine, for that is debauchery, but be filled with the Spirit, addressing one another in psalms and hymns and spiritual songs, singing and making melody to the Lord with your heart, giving thanks always and for everything to God the Father in the name of our Lord Jesus Christ, submitting to one another out of reverence for Christ. Ephesians 5:15-21

Singing songs of praise to God is something we should be doing whether anyone is listening or not, "singing and making melody to the Lord with your heart..." because it one of the ways that God tells us to worship Him. We should also be singing with others, though. The passage says, "addressing one another in psalms and hymns and spiritual songs." That's why we sing in church and why it's a good idea for us to sing as a family.

There is a lot to be learned from singing the songs of the faith. Here's a passage that makes that clear:

Let the word of Christ dwell in you richly, teaching and admonishing one another in all wisdom, singing psalms and hymns and spiritual songs, with thankfulness in your hearts to God. Colossians 3:16

Singing hymns can be part of letting the word of Christ dwell in us and part of teaching and admonishing (that means to warn or advise) one another, too.

That's what we are going to be doing – learning the Christmas carols, but also learning about what they mean and what they can teach us about Jesus.

Come Thou Long Expected Jesus

The Plains of Heaven, John Martin, circa 1851

In the mercy of God, when Adam and Eve sinned against Him and broke fellowship with their Creator, God immediately told them of a coming Savior. From the very earliest times, mankind had this hope of a Redeemer to come. We celebrate His birth at Christmas time!

But believers ever since have looked forward to Jesus' triumphant return. Just as people in the Old Testament had no idea when the Messiah would appear, we of the New Testament age anticipate His second coming – at a time only God the Father knows! (Matthew 24:36)

This song is a prayer to hasten that day! The painting is meant to depict the New Heavens and the New Earth that the Lord will create for His people when

He comes again. How do you think the artist gives the impression of a brand new, perfect world?

The author of this hymn is Charles Wesley, the brother and partner of John Wesley, one of the founders of the Methodist movement. Charles wrote hundreds of hymns, many of which are still in frequent use. He considered it important for the church to remember and celebrate special events in Jesus' life, and in 1745, he published a collection of Christmas hymns -- including this one. Like many of Wesley's hymns, nearly every phrase in this is based on Scripture!

Often the familiar tune to a hymn was adopted many years after the words were composed. The most common melody for this hymn, a Welsh tune called "Hyfrydol," was written by Rowland Prichard a hundred years after Wesley's lyrics. While it grew in popularity through the 1800s, the lack of consensus about a tune prevented this excellent song from being adopted in the *Wesleyan Hymn Book* until 1875.

[Play a midi file with the tune <u>at Hymnary</u> where you can also read more about it.]

Come Thou Long Expected Jesus

*These rich words, from the Old Testament and New, remind us why Jesus came
and is a prayer for Him to come again as our reigning King.*

1. Come, thou long expected Jesus,
    born to set thy people free;
    from our fears and sins release us,
    let us find our rest in thee.

    Israel's strength and consolation,
    hope of all the earth thou art;
    dear desire of every nation,
    joy of every longing heart.

2. Born thy people to deliver,
    born a child and yet a King,
    born to reign in us forever,
    now thy gracious kingdom bring.

    By thine own eternal spirit
    rule in all our hearts alone;
    by thine all sufficient merit,
    raise us to thy glorious throne.

Born to Set Thy People Free

Expulsion from the Garden of Eden, Thomas Cole, 1828

Let's sing *Come Thou Long Expected Jesus* again. Now, let's learn more about it! Today we are going to talk about the first half of the first verse, which is a prayer of invitation to the Lord Jesus Himself! We should sing it with joy and reverence.

Come thou long-expected Jesus,

Born to set thy people free,

From our fears and sins release us,

Let us find our rest in thee:

We frequently look forward to Christmas time, where we experience the love of family, feasts and treats, and the excitement of exchanging presents. Our natural joy in celebrating Christmas grows from the meaning of the day – our joy for the ultimate gift of the Messiah, promised long ago.

Look at the painting for today. Thomas Cole, founder of the Hudson River School – a 19th century style of landscape art, painted Adam and Eve being expelled from the Garden. We see the glory of God shining from the Garden and Adam and Eve fleeing out into the world. Heartbreaking, isn't it? It must have seemed the end of all things to them, but God gave them – and us – hope.

How long have we expected Jesus? All the way back to the Garden of Eden, when God told the serpent, *"I will put enmity ... between your seed and her Seed,"* that is, the descendent of Eve. *"He shall bruise your head, and you shall bruise His heel."* (Genesis 3:15) God promised a Savior to come, the Messiah we now recognize as Jesus.

He was born to set His people free. Jesus explained in the early days of His preaching, *"He [God] has sent Me ... to proclaim liberty to the captives, and the opening of prison to those who are bound."* He was pointing to His mission, foretold in Isaiah 61:1 and quoted by Him in Luke 4:18-19.

What would that freedom look like? When the angel announced the coming Messiah to Joseph, he said, *"you shall call his name Jesus, for He will save His people from their sins."* (Matthew 1:21). And the apostle Paul told the church in Rome, *"For the law of the Spirit of life in Christ Jesus has made me free from the law of sin and death."* (Romans 8:2) Jesus sets His people free from our fears and sins, as Wesley wrote!

And that freedom lifts the burden from our conscience and gives us peace. Jesus said, *"Come to Me, all you who labor and are heavy laden, and I will give you rest.*

Take My yoke upon you and learn from Me, for I am gentle and lowly of heart, and you will find rest for your souls." (Matthew 11:28-29)

One last thing. We don't say "thee" and "thou" today except in religious language – an echo from the King James Version of the Bible. Today, we think these terms add greater dignity to a verse or a ceremony. For an English-speaking believer in the 1600s, though, referring to Jesus as "thou" was addressing Him as a loved family member. English has lost that distinction between the familiar way you speak to friends and family and the more formal "you", but it's still present in many other languages. When you see "thee" and "thou" in hymns and prayers, remember that it's not holding Jesus at a fearful distance – it's drawing Him close like a brother!

Let's pray.

Dear Desire of Every Nation

St Paul Preaching in Athens, Raphael, 1515

Sing the whole carol again. Let's look at the second half of verse one today, where we see the Lord described with phrases from passages in the Word.

Israel's strength and consolation,
Hope of all the earth thou art,
Dear desire of every nation,
Joy of every longing heart.

Christ is Israel's strength and consolation – The promise of a Savior was eagerly held by the Israelites. This phrase actually quotes two verses. In the Old Testament, the prophet Samuel referred to God as *"the **Strength of Israel** [who]* *will not lie nor relent."* Jesus, the Son, carries this in His union with God the Father (remember Jesus said, *"I and My Father are one."* (John 10:30)) – Jesus is also the Strength of Israel. Since he was writing in 1745, Charles Wesley is quoting from the King James Version of the Bible. In that translation, 1 Samuel 15:29 refers to God as "the Strength of Israel"; your modern translation may say, "the Glory of Israel," but Jesus is both.

When Jesus was a newborn, Joseph and Mary took Him to the Temple for His dedication. There they met an elderly man, Simeon, who was *"just and devout, waiting for the Consolation of Israel,"* meaning the promised Messiah. (Luke 2:25). That day, Simeon met his long-expected Savior!

But He is the hope of the Gentiles, too. The next two lines speak about Jesus' care for all people, not just the Israelites. When God blessed Abraham, the ancestor of the Jews, He said, *"In your seed all the nations of the earth shall be blessed"* a promise that was repeated five times (see Genesis 22:18 for one example). Even though there was mistrust and hostility between Jews and Gentiles for much of history, the time would come when both would seek the same Savior!

God told the prophet Isaiah that when the Messiah came, *"He will bring forth justice to the Gentiles,"* He would be *"a light to the Gentiles"* and *"In His name the Gentiles will trust."* (Isaiah 42:1, 6; Matthew 12:21). To the prophet Haggai, God said, *"I will shake all nations, and they shall come to the Desire of All Nations"* – the promised Savior (Haggai 2:7).

When the Savior was born, the angel told the shepherds, *"I bring you good tidings of great joy which shall be to all people."* (Luke 2:10)

So Paul, the great apostle to the Gentiles, wrote that Jesus *"has broken down the middle wall of separation ... that He might reconcile them both to God ... putting to death the enmity."* (Ephesians 2:14, 16) In today's painting, we see Paul preaching to the Greeks at Athens, a group of pagans hearing the gospel for the first time.

This is the promised and expected Messiah who will offer forgiveness and salvation to all nations – Jews and Gentiles alike!

Let's pray.

Born a Child and Yet a King

The Magi Before Herod, Matteo di Giovanni, circa 1490

Born thy people to deliver,

Born a child and yet a king,

Born to reign in us for ever,

Now thy gracious kingdom bring;

Who are Jesus' people? We saw in the first verse that God's grace was extended to both Jew and Gentile. In this verse, we can remember that God's people are called *"out of every tribe and tongue and people and nation."* (Revelation 5:9). Paul told the Galatians, *"You are all sons of God through faith in Jesus Christ ... there is neither Jew nor Greek."* (Galatians 3:26, 28). When we have trusted Christ, each of us can say with the Psalmist, *"I sought the Lord, and He heard me, and delivered me from all my fears."* (Psalm 34:4) and that means we are part of Jesus' people.

A king from the beginning. The wise men from the East sought royalty, a baby born to be king. They followed the star to Israel and went directly to Herod, the ruler, as we see illustrated in today's painting, asking, *"Where is He who is born King of the Jews?"* (Matthew 2:2) They were looking for a child whom they would recognize as a king, even in His cradle! In God's perfect plan, the Son of God did not appear magically, full grown, but took on human flesh and entered the world as a humble baby, just like all of us.

A king forever! The Bible tells us that the Messiah would occupy David's throne – in other words, He would be a king in the line of David's descendents. Unlike David's other sons and grandsons, this One would be ruler forever. *"The Lord God will give Him the throne of His father David ...,"* the angel told Mary, *"and of His kingdom there will be no end."* (Luke 1:32-33)

And like Jesus taught His disciples, we pray for His kingdom to come! (Matthew 6:10)

Doesn't this refer to Jesus' second coming? YES! And this hymn can be sung as joyful thanks for Jesus' birth, and hopeful expectation of His return. We can experience a foretaste – something of an appetizer – of God's kingdom on earth, and look forward to the full banquet of His kingdom in heaven!

Let's pray.

Raise Us to Thy Glorious Throne

Glory of Saints, Corrado Giaquinto, 1755-1756

By thine own eternal Spirit
Rule in all our hearts alone,
By thine all-sufficient merit
Raise us to thy glorious throne.

A spiritual kingdom. When Jesus stood before Pontius Pilate, the Roman asked if He was a king. Jesus affirmed that He is, but He told Pilate, "*My kingdom is not of this world.*" (John 18:33-37)

Jesus' kingdom crosses all boundaries and barriers, because He rules in our hearts through the Holy Spirit. We receive the Spirit when we believe, and Jesus dwells within us through the Spirit. He alone rules in our hearts. One day, though, His Kingdom will be visible to everyone.

By thine all sufficient merit raise us to thy glorious throne. On our own, we can never deserve the gift of eternal life; we are sinners and our sin separates us from God. Romans 3 tells us, "for all have sinned and fall short of the glory of God," and we can never earn God's forgiveness by our own merit, or worthiness.

Jesus, however, lived a life of perfect obedience to God; He never sinned. Because of His moral perfection, Jesus could voluntarily take the punishment which each of us deserves. His righteousness actually merits God's favor – and Jesus' righteousness is a gift to all who trust Him in faith. Only Jesus' merit is sufficient to save us from our sins!

When we have received God's forgiveness through the sacrifice of Jesus, we receive the Holy Spirit in this life and our welcome into heaven when we die.

And God both raised up the Lord and will also raise us up by His power (1 Corinthians 6:14)

Now, therefore, you are no longer strangers and foreigners, but fellow citizens with the saints and members of the household of God. (Ephesians 2:19) We'll be welcomed into Christ's Kingdom just like all the saints, which is just another word for those sanctified by Christ's blood. In today's painting, we see Moses in the middle pointing up to the glorious light and below him Abraham and Isaac with the lamb God provided. On one side is King David and famous women of the Bible and on the other more modern saints. Because of Jesus' sacrifice, we'll join all the believers of every nation and time, praising God forever more!

Let's pray.

Joy to the World

Annunciation to the Shepherds, Joachim Wtewael, 1606

This familiar song may be the most popular Christmas hymn in the English language! The words are by Isaac Watts, an English pastor who wrote over 750 hymns, many of which are still in use today. This triumphant song is inspired by Psalm 98, which calls all of Creation to rejoice in God's work of salvation.

Sometimes when we sing without a recording or an instrument, it's hard to choose the note to start on. "Joy to the World" is really easy – it's exactly one octave in range. What's an octave? That's a full scale – remember in The Sound of Music where they sang "do-re-mi-fa-so-la-ti-do"? In this song, the verse starts on the high end of the octave, "Joy" – and goes all the way down to the bottom of the scale, "come." If you can comfortably sing the first line, you can sing the whole song!

Joy to the world; the Lord is come;
Let earth receive her King:
Let every heart prepare Him room,
And heaven and nature sing
And heaven and nature sing
And heaven, and heaven and nature sing

The first verse calls all the world to rejoice in Jesus' arrival. This could mean "all the people of the world," or "the whole created world itself." As we'll see, the hymn really means both!

In our modern times, especially countries based on elections and constitutional government, we don't really appreciate what a true monarch means. Jesus was not elected by voters; His authority does not rest on popular opinion; He is not subject to a recall or vote of no confidence. Jesus is born as the king of all the earth, the ultimate ruler – the King of all other kings – but unlike other kings, Jesus is always perfectly good. He is always just, always kind, always wise. We can trust Him without hesitation!

The arrival of this King is a time for rejoicing! Both heaven and the created world are called to celebrate, and humankind are called to invite Him in. Psalm

98 calls, *"Shout joyfully to the Lord, all the earth; break forth into song, rejoice, and sing praises."* (Psalm 98:4)

Of course, in the Christmas story we read of the songs of angels filling the heavens, but the Bible also speaks of the natural world praising God as well. God told Isaiah, *"The beast of the field will honor Me, the jackals and the ostriches."* (Isaiah 43:20). And Psalm 98 continues, *"Let the sea roar, and all its fulness."* In the painting for today, even the sheep and dogs are captivated by the angels and the glory.

Even heavenly bodies, natural forces, and weather are called to praise God – *"Praise Him, sun and moon; praise Him, all you stars of light! ... Fire and hail, snow and clouds; stormy wind, fulfilling His word ... Let them praise the name of the Lord."* (Psalm 148:3, 8, 13)

Does this suggest that animals and planets speak out in literal voices? No – but we see God's wisdom displayed in their complexity and beauty, and their orderly patterns and instinctive behaviors all speak of the power of the One who formed them from nothing. Psalm 19 says, *"The heavens declare the glory of God, and the firmament shows His handiwork."* When we look at Creation, we see evidence of a Creator all around us.

So, created things witness to the wonderful God who rules the earth!

Let's sing the whole carol, then pray!

[Play a midi file with the tune at Hymnary where you can also read more about it.]

Joy to the World

This carol calls all of Creation to join the song of praise.

Joy to the world; the Lord is come;
Let earth receive her King:
Let every heart prepare Him room,
And heaven and nature sing
And heaven and nature sing
And heaven, and heaven and nature sing

Joy to the earth, the Savior reigns;
Let men their songs employ;
While fields and floods, rocks, hills and plains,
Repeat the sounding joy
Repeat the sounding joy
Repeat, repeat the sounding joy

No more let sins and sorrows grow,
Nor thorns infest the ground;
He comes to make His blessings flow,
Far as the curse is found
Far as the curse is found
Far as, far as the curse is found.

He rules the world with truth and grace,
And makes the nations prove
The glories of His righteousness
And wonders of His love
And wonders of His love
And wonders, wonders of His love

Let Men Their Songs Employ

A Christmas Carol in Lucerne, Hans Bachmann, 1887

Joy to the earth, the Savior reigns;

Let men their songs employ;

While fields and floods, rocks, hills and plains,

Repeat the sounding joy

Repeat the sounding joy

Repeat, repeat the sounding joy

Sing the whole carol again, then we'll talk about the second verse, where we learn more about this new King – He is also the Savior (more about that later).

Isaac Watts was inspired by Psalm 98, but that chapter is surrounded by several other psalms of praise toward God. For example, Psalm 96 says, "O sing to the Lord a new song! Sing to the Lord, all the earth. Sing to the Lord, bless His name; proclaim the good news of His salvation from day to day." Psalm 97 declares, "The Lord reigns; let the earth rejoice …"

And as all of mankind rejoices for our kind and loving King, the rest of the created world echoes back our song. You see how the hymn brings the Scriptural references into the song. "Let the field be joyful and all that is in it," (Psalm 96:12) "Let the floods clap their hands: let the hills be joyful together," (Psalm 98:8 KJV) and "the little hills rejoice on every side. The pastures are clothed with flocks; the valleys also are covered with grain; they shout for joy, they also sing." (Psalm 65:12-13)

And like Jesus told the Pharisees, if His disciples kept quiet, "the stones would immediately cry out" in His praise. (Luke 19:40) While fields and floods, rocks, hills, and plains repeat the sounding joy, as this verse has it.

Did you know people have been caroling, singing Christmas hymns from house to house, for over 700 years? It started with St. Francis of Assisi, who encouraged his parishioners to sing at Christmas and continued over the centuries with singing, well-wishes, and shared hospitality. Today's painting illustrates carolers singing at a home in Lucerne, Switzerland in the 19th century. Our own family has a caroling party every year. Have you ever been caroling? It's a wonderful way to share the gospel with your community.

Let's pray!

He Comes to Make His Blessings Flow

Adam and Eve Expelled from Paradise, Gustave Doré, 1865

No more let sins and sorrows grow,

Nor thorns infest the ground;

He comes to make His blessings flow,

Far as the curse is found

Far as the curse is found

Far as, far as the curse is found.

The third verse reminds us why we need this Savior-King – because of our natural state of sin and separation from God.

When our first parents, Adam and Eve, lived in a perfect world with daily, face-to-face conversation with their Creator, their decision to disobey God's simple commandment was an act of cosmic insurrection! Our artwork today is a woodcut from Gustave Doré that shows them being cast out of the Garden of Eden into a fallen world full of thorns and trials.

All our sorrows today are the result of sin entering the world through mankind's rebellion. Even the natural world around us suffers from the effects of sin. "The creation was subjected to futility," Paul explained, "We know that the whole creation groans and labors with birth pangs together until now." (Romans 8:20, 22) One example of that is the growth of harmful and frustrating things in nature. God told Adam that because of his disobedience, "Cursed is the ground for your sake … Both thorns and thistles it shall bring forth for you." (Genesis 3:17-18) His work of tending the soil became hard and unproductive because of the power of sin.

But the Bible also tells us there will be a restoration and healing when the Lord returns. "For the earnest expectation of the creation eagerly waits for the revealing of the sons of God," we read. "The creation itself will be delivered from the bondage of corruption into the glorious liberty of the children of God." (Romans 8:19, 21)

And our human sorrows will end as well. When Jesus returns to gather His people to His kingdom, "then shall be brought to pass the saying that is written, 'Death is swallowed up in victory. O death, where is thy sting? O grave, where is thy victory?'" (1 Corinthians 15:54-55 KJV)

The final book of the Bible describes the blessing of God's never-ending heaven. "And God will wipe away every tear from their eyes; there will be no more death, nor sorrow, nor crying. There shall be no more pain, for the former things have passed away." (Revelation 21:4)

So, Christ's reign on earth will overcome the sin which kills, and His gracious rule will banish the painful and unfruitful thorns (both in our fields and our hearts!) as far and wide as Adam's curse has reached. What a blessing to look forward to the elimination of sickness, poverty, suffering of any kind, and even death itself. Joy to the world, indeed! Let's pray.

The Glories of His Righteousness

The Baptism of the Eunuch, Rembrandt van Rijn, 1626

He rules the world with truth and grace,

And makes the nations prove

The glories of His righteousness

And wonders of His love

And wonders of His love

And wonders, wonders of His love

Sing the carol, then let's look at the fourth verse. The Gospel of John speaks of the coming of Jesus, the son of God, born into human kind. "And the Word became flesh and dwelt among us, and we beheld His glory, the glory as of the only begotten of the Father, full of grace and truth." (John 1:14)

And while Jesus was sent first to the people of Israel, it was always God's plan to include the Gentiles in His heavenly kingdom. "The Lord has made known His salvation; His righteousness He has revealed in the sight of the nations." (Psalm 98:2) When the Bible speaks about "nations," it usually means the non-Jewish peoples outside of God's chosen people of Israel.

One of the messages of the New Testament is God's invitation to all people. In the book of Revelation, the Lamb of God – Jesus – is praised for providing salvation to believers "out of every tribe and tongue and people and nation." (Revelation 5:9) As Peter told the first Gentile converts to faith in Christ, "In truth I perceive that God shows no partiality. But in every nation whoever fears Him and works righteousness is accepted by Him." (Acts 10:34-35)

A great example of that is found in the story of the Ethiopian eunuch in Acts chapter 8 and illustrated in Rembrandt's painting above. The Holy Spirit led Philip, one of the disciples, to the exact spot where he would meet a court official of the Queen of Ethiopia who was reading the Word of God, but not understanding what he was reading. Philip explained the gospel and the eunuch was converted!

Now, God has shown that "there is no distinction between Jew and Greek, for the same Lord over all is rich to all who call upon Him. For 'whoever calls on the name of the Lord shall be saved.'" (Romans 10:12-13) So whether we are children of Abraham, Isaac, and Jacob, or our ancestry comes from "the nations," God extends a gracious invitation to come to Him in faith!

Let's pray!

Psalms and Hymns and Spiritual Songs

Coro De Ninos (Choir Boys), Jose Rico y Cejudo, circa 1890

The Bible tells us that singing is part of our worship of God, and those songs may take many different forms. Paul wrote to the church at Colosse, "Let the word of Christ dwell in you richly in all wisdom; teaching and admonishing one another in psalms and hymns and spiritual songs, singing with grace in your hearts to the Lord." (Colossians 3:16)

Church music has undergone many changes since that was written almost two thousand years ago. During the Middle Ages, singing in churches was only conducted in Latin. Many times, young choir boys, as pictured in today's art, sang the soprano parts. After the Reformation, whole congregations began singing and in their native tongues.

For many years, the English-speaking Protestant churches sang almost nothing but psalms, revised to fit English poetic forms which are easier to sing. A few of these are still in our hymnbooks today, like "All People That On Earth Do Dwell" – a musical setting of Psalm 100.

However, a revolution in church music came about in the 1700's. Isaac Watts (1674-1748) published his version of the psalms in 1719, with the title The Psalms of David, Imitated in the Language of the New Testament. "Joy to the World" appears on page 44 based on Psalm 98.

Watts realized that many of the things written in King David's time had been further explained by the life and teaching of Jesus. As he worked on his collection of psalms, Watts wrote, "Where the Psalmist describes religion by the fear of God, I have often joined faith and love to it. Where he speaks of the pardon of sin, through the mercies of God, I have added the merits of a Saviour." Instead of only looking for a future Messiah, like the Old Testament psalms do, Watts' hymns look back to the birth and life of Jesus with thankfulness, and look forward to His future return and kingdom. "Joy to the World" captures both arrivals of God's Son!

Besides the psalms, Watts wrote many hymns which are still sung today, like "Jesus Shall Reign," "O God Our Help in Ages Past," and "When I Survey the Wondrous Cross." His hymns were meant to express the faith of Christians. His very Biblical texts helped convince churches in Britain and America to embrace "hymns and spiritual songs," as well as the psalms, as mentioned in Paul's letters. For a time, Watts' hymns were the only ones sung in some churches! Because of his tremendous influence – and the fact he wrote over 600 hymns – Isaac Watts is called "The Father of English Hymnody."

Let's look at how Watts used Psalm 98 into create "Joy to the World."

Psalm 98:4-9 (KJV)

4 Make a joyful noise unto the Lord, all the earth: make a loud noise, and rejoice, and sing praise

5 Sing unto the Lord with the harp; with the harp, and the voice of a psalm.

6 With trumpets and the sound of a cornet make a joyful noise before the Lord, the King.

7 Let the sea roar, and the fulness thereof; the world, and they that dwell therein.

8 Let the floods clap their hands: let the hills be joyful together

9 Before the Lord; for he cometh to judge the earth: with righteousness shall he judge the world, and the people with equity.

Let's pray.

Joy to the World by Isaac Watts

Joy to the world, the Lord is come
Let earth receive her king
Let ev'ry heart prepare Him room
And heaven and nature sing

Joy to the earth, the Savior reigns
Let men their songs employ

While fields and floods, rocks, hills, and plains
Repeat the sounding joy.

No more let sins and sorrows grow
Nor thorns infest the ground
He comes to make His blessings flow
Far as the curse is found.

He rules the world with truth and grace
And makes the nations prove
The glories of His righteousness
And wonders of His love.

O Come, O Come Emmanuel

The Flight of the Prisoners, Joseph Tissot, circa 1896-1902

This carol brings to mind monks singing Gregorian chants for a good reason! In Medieval times, monks would sing vespers every evening. In the last week of Advent, after they sang the *Magnificat* (based on Mary's prayer in Luke 1:46–55), they would add *O Antiphons,* verses beginning with the word "O" that mentioned names for Jesus in Scripture. This carol was originally a collection of these separate verses which were finally put together as a hymn of its own.

"O Come, O Come Emmanuel" is a translation by John Mason Neale (1818-1866) of that Latin hymn, *Veni, Veni, Emmanuel*. Neale was an Anglican priest and a classical scholar, known for trying to rejuvenate Anglican worship by translating ancient hymns from Latin, Greek and other languages.

The words date back to the 8th or 9th century – over 1200 years ago! The tune is a type of plainsong or plainchant that monks would sing in unison, instead of in harmony. The words were not put with the tune until 1851, when Neale published his first version of the song. The words we'll study this week come from his revision for the 1861 hymnbook, *Hymns Ancient and Modern*. Many people sing the verses in unison, then break into harmony for the chorus.

Besides this hymn, Neale is also known for many other translations. The Palm Sunday hymn All Glory, Laud, and Honor is another with Latin roots, while Good King Wenceslas was translated from a poem in Czech.

Let's look at the first verse of O Come, O Come, Emmanuel.

O come, O come, Emmanuel
And ransom captive Israel
That mourns in lowly exile here
Until the Son of God appear
Rejoice! Rejoice! Emmanuel
Shall come to thee, O Israel

Ever since our first parents left the Garden of Eden, there has been a longing for the Redeemer which God had promised. What's more, God had said the Messiah would be more than a great man. The prophet Isaiah had said, "Behold, the virgin shall conceive and bear a Son, and shall call His name Immanuel"; the gospel of Matthew quotes the prophecy and continues, "which is translated, 'God with us.'" (Isaiah 7:14 and Matthew 1:23).

This hymn helps us remember the long years of hope and expectation before Jesus' birth. God had blessed Israel's forefather Abraham and promised Him a country for his descendants (Genesis 13:14-17). The Israelites lived in that land for a time, but when they turned away from God, they were carried away as prisoners to distant countries (2 Kings 18:11-12). For many years, Israel was literally exiled from the land which God promised. Today's art illustrates the Israelites leaving Jerusalem for exile in Babylon.

A redeemer is someone who pays the penalty to set a prisoner free. The song says "ransom," and that's what Jesus is to Israel, the Redeemer who purchases their freedom – and for all His people, from every time and place! When we realize our need of a Savior, someone to pay for our sins and offer us forgiveness, we can all, Jews and Gentiles, look to the Messiah who already came, just like the ancient Israelites looked forward to the Messiah yet to come. Sometimes people sing the last verse with the refrain, "*Has* come to thee, O Israel."

Why is Emmanuel spelled with an "I" sometimes and an "E" other times? When you translate from one language to another, sometimes you have to make a decision about how to spell names in the new language. Isaiah wrote in Hebrew; when Matthew quoted him in Greek, which uses a different alphabet, he spelled the name with an "E". Our English Bibles go back to the original Hebrew and use the "I" spelling, but since Neale was translating from a Latin hymn which used words from the Latin Vulgate Bible, translated into Latin from the Greek, he used the "E" which he found there.

Let's pray.

[Play a midi file with the tune at Hymnary where you can also read more about it.]

O Come, O Come Emmanuel

This ancient hymn dates back nearly 1200 years.

O come, O come, Emmanuel
And ransom captive Israel
That mourns in lowly exile here
Until the Son of God appear
    Rejoice! Rejoice! Emmanuel
    Shall come to thee, O Israel

O come, Thou Rod of Jesse, free
Thine own from Satan's tyrrany;
From depths of Hell Thy people
save,
And give them victory o'er the
grave.
    Rejoice! Rejoice! Emmanuel
    Shall come to thee, O Israel

O come, Thou Day-Spring, come and
cheer
Thy people by Thine Advent here;
Disperse the gloomy clouds of night,
And death's dark shadows put to
flight.
    Rejoice! Rejoice! Emmanuel
    Shall come to thee, O Israel

O come, Thou Key of David, come
And open wide our heavenly Home;
Make safe the way that leads on high
And close the path to misery.
    Rejoice! Rejoice! Emmanuel
    Shall come to thee, O Israel

O come, O come, Thou Lord of Might
Who to Thy tribes, on Sinai's height
In ancient times didst give the Law
In Cloud, and Majesty, and Awe.
    Rejoice! Rejoice! Emmanuel
    Shall come to thee, O Israel

In Ancient Times Didst Give the Law

Moses Presenting the Tablets of the Law, Philippe de Champaigne, circa 1648.jpg

O come, O come, Thou Lord of Might

Who to Thy tribes, on Sinai's height

In ancient times didst give the Law

In Cloud, and Majesty, and Awe.

Rejoice! Rejoice! Emmanuel

Shall come to thee, O Israel

Let's sing the whole carol, then talk about verse 2. The Jewish believer looking forward to Emmanuel, "God with Us," would naturally think of God as he knew him then. Isaiah 33:22 says, "For the Lord is our Judge; the Lord is our Lawgiver; the Lord is our King; He will save us."

The reference to Sinai, of course, is the giving of the Ten Commandments, the most fundamental law of God's people, on that mountain in the wilderness (Exodus 20:1-20). When God met with Moses to reveal His laws, "there were thunderings and lightnings, and a thick cloud on the mountain ... Mount Sinai was completely in smoke ... and the whole mountain quaked greatly." (Exodus 19:16, 18)

That was pretty dramatic! The Bible tells us, "When the people saw it, they trembled and stood afar off. Then they said to Moses, 'You speak to us, and we will hear; but let not God speak to us, lest we die.'" (Exodus 20:18-19) No surprise there! In the painting today, we see a representation of Moses presenting the tablets of the law. One interesting thing to note is that the law is written in French! It's common for classical painters to illustrate biblical scenes as if they happened in their native lands. It probably isn't ignorance since Europeans even many years ago were very familiar with the culture of the Middle East. We don't think it's some kind of cultural superiority, either. We think it's probably that the Word of God is universal! The Bible applies to all of us in every culture. When we hear the stories, they feel very familiar and it's natural to imagine them happening among people just like us. The painter made that law very personal to his viewers by writing it in their language.

Now that Jesus has come, our interaction with God has changed. "For you have not come to the mountain that may be touched and that burned with fire ... so terrifying was the sight that Moses said, 'I am exceedingly afraid and trembling' – but instead, "to Jesus the Mediator of the new covenant." (Hebrews 12:18, 21, 24) Paul explains, "You did not receive the spirit of bondage again to fear, but you received the Spirit of adoption by whom we cry out, 'Abba, Father.'" (Romans 8:15)

What a difference, when "God with Us" is more than the fearsome coming of the Judge and Lawgiver, but the arrival of a loving Father. Jesus said, "Do not think that I came to destroy the Law or the Prophets. I did not come to destroy but to fulfill." (Matthew 5:17) But God's holy commandments are more than we can bear, because Jesus said, "Unless your righteousness exceed the righteousness of the scribes and Pharisees," the most careful and scrupulous Jews of them all, "you will by no means enter the kingdom of heaven." (Matthew 5:20)

Instead, we now understand that "The law was our tutor to lead us to Christ," (Galatians 3:24), and that "Christ is the end [or goal] of the law for righteousness to everyone who believes." (Romans 10:4). We can't achieve sinless perfection ourselves, "For all have sinned and fall short of the glory of God," (Romans 3:23), but Jesus fully kept God's law for us. Jesus "condemned sin in the flesh, that the righteous requirement of the law might be fulfilled in us" (Romans 8:3-4), and because of this, "There is therefore now no condemnation for those who are in Christ Jesus." (Romans 8:1) That is really something to rejoice over, so sing out when you get to the refrain!

Let's pray.

O Come, Thou Rod of Jesse

King David Playing the Harp, Gerard van Honthorst, 1622

O come, Thou Rod of Jesse, free
Thine own from Satan's tyranny;
From depths of Hell Thy people save,
And give them victory o'er the grave.
Rejoice! Rejoice! Emmanuel
Shall come to thee, O Israel

God told King David that one of his descendants would be a king that ruled forever (2 Samuel 7:12-13). For centuries, the Jews looked for the promised Son of David, and when Jesus appeared in public, He was often identified as the Son.

The prophet Isaiah spoke of the Messiah, saying, "There shall come forth a Rod from the stem of Jesse, and a Branch shall grow out of his roots … the Gentiles shall seek Him, and His resting place shall be glorious." (Isaiah 11:1, 10) Jesse, you may remember, was the father of David (Ruth 4:22), so Jesus who descended from David also descended from David's father.

Today's painting is of King David. Did you know that David was a musician as well as a king and wrote many of the Psalms? That's why he is often portrayed with a musical instrument.

Jesus said that "Whoever commits sin is a slave of sin," (John 8:34), and Paul said that those who pursue sin have fallen into "the snare of the devil, having been taken captive by him to do his will." (2 Timothy 2:26) But Jesus died to save His people from their sins, and also "that through death He might destroy him who had the power of death, that is, the devil, and release those who through fear of death were all their lifetime subject to bondage." (Matthew 1:21 and Hebrews 2:14-15)

The next line may be confusing: From depths of Hell Thy people save. The original Latin clearly means a place of punishment, but the Bible says that It is appointed for men to die once, but after this the judgement. (Hebrews 9:27) Our souls don't change location in the afterlife! What is meant here is that Jesus' salvation takes us off our pathway to Hell and rescues us from the punishment we deserve. When we know that forgiveness, we no longer need to fear death (Hebrews 2:15, above!). When we have that relationship with Jesus, Paul wrote,

Death is swallowed up in victory. O death, where is thy sting? O grave, where is thy victory? The sting of death is sin; and the strength of sin is the law. But thanks be to God, which giveth us the victory through our Lord Jesus Christ. (1 Corinthians 15:54-57, KJV)

What great news that is! Let's pray.

Death's Dark Shadows Put to Flight

Zacharias Writes Down the Name of his Son, Domenico Ghirlandaio, circa 1490

O come, Thou Day-Spring, come and cheer
Thy people by Thine Advent here;
Disperse the gloomy clouds of night,
And death's dark shadows put to flight.
Rejoice! Rejoice! Emmanuel
Shall come to thee, O Israel

The first line addresses Jesus as the Dayspring. This is from the prophecy spoken by Zecharias, the father of John the Baptist, speaking of his son's mission as the Forerunner to the Messiah (Luke 1:67-79, NKJV) – the One who would call Himself "the Bright and Morning Star." (Revelation 22:16)

Today's art is a fresco showing Zecharias writing down the name of his son who would become John the Baptist. You might remember that he was mute (unable to speak) from the time he received the prophecy of the birth from the angel until he named that baby John. (Luke 1)

The Bible is full of the contrast of light and darkness. Sometimes it's innocent and natural, like the alternation of daytime and nighttime which God established at Creation (Genesis 1:4-5).

In many places, though, darkness is symbolic of fear and evil, sin and death. The Bible says that when people refused to honor God and give Him thanks, "they became futile in their thoughts, and their foolish hearts were darkened." (Romans 1:21) Psalm 107 speaks of "Those who sat in darkness and the shadow of death, bound in affliction and irons, because they rebelled against the words of God and despised the counsel of the Most High." (Psalm 107:10-11) So much of this is self-inflicted, the result of turning away from God's goodness. "Men loved darkness rather than light, because their deeds were evil." (John 3:19)

God did not leave us without hope, though. He told the prophet Isaiah, speaking of the promised Messiah, "behold, darkness shall cover the earth, and deep darkness the people; but the Lord will arise over you, and His glory will be seen upon you." (Isaiah 60:2) God said in the last book of the Old Testament, "To you who fear my name, the Sun of Righteousness shall arise with healing in His wings." (Malachi 4:2) When the Messiah comes, it will be said, "The people who walked in darkness have seen a great light; those who dwelt in the land of the shadow of death, upon them a light has shined." (Isaiah 9:2)

And Jesus Himself said, "I am the light of the world. He who follows Me shall not walk in darkness, but have the light of life." (John 8:12) As Christ-followers, we know that "He has delivered us from the power of darkness and conveyed us into the kingdom of the Son of His love," (Colossians 1:13) ... and death's shadows are put to flight!

Let's pray.

Open Wide Our Heavenly Home

The Nativity with the Prophets Isaiah and Ezekiel, Duccio di Buoninsegna 1308-1311

O come, Thou Key of David, come
And open wide our heavenly Home;
Make safe the way that leads on high
And close the path to misery.
Rejoice! Rejoice! Emmanuel
Shall come to thee, O Israel

The Messianic prophecy in Isaiah says, "Unto us a child is born, unto us a Son is given; and the government will be upon His shoulder." (Isaiah 9:6) The Jews understood this would be the continuation of the house of David, as God had promised – "I will set up your seed after you, who will come from your body, and I will establish the throne of his kingdom forever." (2 Samuel 7:12) – and the coming Messiah would be called the Son of David (Matthew 1:1). Our art for today places the prophets Isaiah and Ezekiel on either side of the Nativity showing that the birth of Jesus was the fulfillment of a great body of prophecy.

This verse focuses on the rule of the eternal king, "He who is holy, He who is true, He who has the key of David, He who opens and no one shuts, and shuts and no one opens." – how Jesus describes Himself in Revelation 3:7!

One of the blessings of trusting Jesus is security. When we place our faith in Christ alone, He promises to keep us in His care. "My sheep hear My voice," Jesus said, "... and I give them eternal life, and they shall never perish; neither shall anyone snatch them out of My hand." (John 10:27-28) We are taken off "the path to misery" and placed instead on the road to "our heavenly home ... on high." "Our citizenship is in heaven," Paul said (Philippians 3:20), and Jesus has prepared a place for His followers – and promised our welcome there! (John 14:2-3)

When we think of our way to heaven being "safe," we remember that doesn't mean we will never have difficulty or sorrow. Jesus Himself told us that – "In the world you will have tribulation," – that's trouble, and big trouble, too! – "but be of good cheer, I have overcome the world." (John 16:33). Our God and Savior said, "I will never leave you nor forsake you," and we can trust that 'The Lord is my helper; I will not fear; what can man do to me?'" (Hebrews 13:5-6). Our way is safe because our arrival is guaranteed!

You might notice that this verse includes two imperfect rhymes. Sometimes a poem doesn't exactly rhyme at the end of lines. "Come" and "Home", in the first two lines, look the same when written but they aren't pronounced the same. Sometimes the rhymes aren't even close – like "high" and "misery." Should you sing the last word as "miser-eye"? We don't think so – we'd recommend just sing it as written and let the hymn's story unfold!

Let's pray!

God Rest You Merry, Gentlemen

The Nativity, Federico Barocci, 1597

God rest you merry, gentlemen,

Let nothing you dismay,

Remember Christ our Savior

Was born upon this day,

To save us all from Satan's pow'r

When we were gone astray,

    O tidings of comfort and joy,

Comfort and joy,
O tidings of comfort and joy!

Although it's not very common in hymnbooks, this is a Christmas song with Biblical references, so it's worth learning and discussing. It's also full of old language which is often misunderstood, so let's get busy!

This is a traditional English folk song with no claim to authorship. One collector of Christmas songs said that every town seemed to have slightly different versions, which is typical of true folk music. One form of the words appeared in print in the 1650s; an arrangement of the familiar tune was published in 1815 by Samuel Wesley, the son of Charles Wesley, the English preacher and hymnwriter.

The first line is "God rest you merry, gentlemen." The phrase is found in some of Shakespeare's plays from the 1590s; the Oxford English Dictionary says it means, "May God grant you peace and happiness." The word "merry" doesn't refer to the gentlemen! If you find this surprising, don't worry; printers were putting the comma in the wrong place as early as 1775, so you're not alone.

It's also common to say, "God rest ye merry", but English scholars point out that's the wrong use for "ye" – it's made-up to sound more archaic.

Before we talk about the verse, let's look at today's art. The joy in this depiction of Mary kneeling before her newborn Son and Savior has makes this a remarkable painting. Notice how the artist used color, light, and shadow to make his point.

Some versions of this carol say, "Christ our Savior / Was born on Christmas Day." To be honest, we don't know precisely what date Jesus' birth occurred. The Romans celebrated the "rebirth" of the sun on the winter solstice, and it seems that early church leadership chose that date, December 25, as the appropriate time to remember the birth of "the Sun of Righteousness," Jesus the Messiah (Malachi 4:2). This is documented as early as AD 336, and it's been on our calendars ever since!

This verse tells us to "remember Christ our Savior..." and that is exactly what the Christmas babe is to us. Jesus came to save His people from their sins (Matthew 1:21) and to destroy the works of the devil (1 John 3:8). And we all need His salvation, because "the whole world lies under the sway of the wicked one" (1 John 5:10) and "There is none righteous, no, not one" (Romans 3:10, Psalm 14:3). That's why this verse tells us that Jesus came "To save us all from Satan's pow'r When we were gone astray."

When the prophet Isaiah says, "All we, like sheep, have gone astray; we have turned, every one, to his own way" (Isaiah 53:6), what tidings (news) of comfort and joy to know Jesus said, "I am the good shepherd, and I know My sheep ... and I lay down My life for the sheep." (John 10:14-15)

As you sing this song, you might notice that there are a few strange accent marks. Let's look at the second verse. When you say the word "blessed" you might normally pronounce it "blest"or "blesd" but the accent mark in "blessed" tells us to pronounce it "bless-ED." Similarly, in the third verse, you would usually pronounce "rejoiced" as "re-joist," but the accent mark in "rejoiced" tells us to pronounced it "re-jois-ED." The changes in pronunciation help the words to fit the music better.

[You can listen to a Midi file of the tune at Hymnary and learn more about the carol, too!]

Let's pray!

God Rest You Merry, Gentlemen

Truly a song of comfort and joy!

God rest you merry, gentlemen,
Let nothing you dismay,
Remember Christ our Savior
Was born upon this day,
To save us all from Satan's pow'r
When we were gone astray,
> *Refrain*
> O tidings of comfort and joy,
> Comfort and joy,
> O tidings of comfort and joy!

From God our heavenly Father
A blessèd angel came,
And unto certain shepherds
Brought tidings of the same,
How that in Bethlehem was born
The Son of God by name,
> *Refrain*

"Fear not," then said the angel,
"Let nothing you affright,
This day is born a Savior
Of a pure Virgin bright,
To free all those who trust in Him
From Satan's power and might,
> *Refrain*

The shepherds at those tidings
Rejoicèd much in mind
And left their flocks a-feeding
In tempest, storm, and wind,
And went to Bethlehem straightway
The Son of God to find,
> *Refrain*

Now to the Lord sing praises,
All you within this place,
And with true love and brotherhood
Each other now embrace,
This holy tide of Christmas
All others doth deface,
> *Refrain*

God bless the ruler of this house,
and send him long to reign,
And many a merry Christmas may
live to see again;
Among your friends and kindred
that live both far and near—
That God send you a happy new
year, happy new year, And God send
you a happy new year.

A Blessèd Angel Came

The Annunciation to the Shepherds, Benjamin Gerritsz Cuyp, Before 1652

From God our heavenly Father
A blessèd angel came,
And unto certain shepherds
Brought tidings of the same,
How that in Bethlehem was born
The Son of God by name,
    O tidings of comfort and joy,
    Comfort and joy,
    O tidings of comfort and joy!

At Christmas time we hear a lot about angels. Of course, they have a dramatic part in the story of Christ's birth. An angel told the virgin Mary that she would be the mother of God's Son (Luke 1:26-38), and told Joseph her fiancé to go ahead and marry her, that the baby she carried was the promised Messiah (Matthew 1:18-25). When the time came for Jesus' birth, the skies over Bethlehem were full of angels rejoicing as you see in today's painting! There may have been more visible angels that year than most of Biblical history.

Angels are God's messengers – in fact, the word comes from the Greek term for a messenger, and sometimes the word is used for clearly human heralds and couriers – not just the heavenly sort. In these accounts around the birth of the Savior, the angels are spiritual beings. Sometimes they appear in human form, but they are not human – and never were.

In the fields around Bethlehem, on the night Jesus was born, a particular angel made the announcement to the shepherds that the Son of God had arrived. Why Bethlehem? We read in Luke's gospel that, due to a census undertaken by the government, Joseph and Mary had traveled from Nazareth to the place of Joseph's ancestors (Luke 2:1-5). As it happened, Joseph was descended from King David (Matthew 1:1-16), who grew up tending sheep near the village of Bethlehem himself! (1 Samuel 17:12, 15)

And the angel came to certain shepherds; they weren't just witnesses to a display of God's glory, or eavesdropping a broadcast announcement to the whole world. Shepherds were not high-status people in Judean society; it was work that could be handled by boys without education or wealth. Yet instead of notifying the Judean king or the Roman commander, God sent His glorious messenger with the world changing news to a specific group of tired men and boys, guarding sheep on the night shift under the stars (Luke 2:8-9). It's true, as God says elsewhere – "As the heavens are higher than the earth, so are My ways higher than your ways, and My thoughts than your thoughts." (Isaiah 55:9) Let's pray.

Fear Not

The Annunciation to the Shepherds, Adam Pynacker, circa 1640

"Fear not," then said the angel,
"Let nothing you affright,
This day is born a Savior
Of a pure Virgin bright,
To free all those who trust in Him
From Satan's power and might,
    O tidings of comfort and joy,
    Comfort and joy
    O tidings of comfort and joy!

It's interesting to note how frequently, when God interacts with man – whether directly from heaven, through His angels, or by the voice of His Son – the encouragement, "Fear not!" comes up. Certainly, in this case, when the quiet and calm of a dark country night was suddenly changed:

"Now there were in the same country shepherds living out in the fields, keeping watch over their flock by night. And behold, an angel of the Lord stood before them, and the glory of the Lord shone around them, and they were greatly afraid." (Luke 2:8-9) Notice the shepherd beginning to run away in the painting.

And sure enough, the angel's first words were, "Do not be afraid!" (Luke 2:10) The King James Version, used when the song was written, uses the traditional phrase "Fear not!" The song repeats the encouragement for good measure – "Let nothing you affright" – an old way of saying, "Let nothing frighten you."

The news is "good tidings of great joy", that nearby in Bethlehem, "the city of David", is the new born Savior, "Christ the Lord." The term "Christ" means "anointed one," which is to say, the promised Messiah from God.

The angel doesn't mention it in His announcement, but the song is correct to recall that Christ is born to a virgin, as the prophecy foretold 700 years before – "Behold, the virgin shall conceive and bear a Son, and shall call His name Immanuel" – which Matthew explains, means "God with us." (Isaiah 7:14, Matthew 1:23)

This newborn Redeemer would take our sins on Himself and give His righteousness to us, so that we could be in a right relationship with God. "My sheep hear My voice," He said later, "and I know them, and they follow Me. And I give them eternal life, and they shall never perish; neither shall anyone snatch them out of My hand." (John 10:27-28). And when we are in the hand of our Lord, "neither death nor life, ... nor any other created thing, shall be able to separate us from the love of God ..." (Romans 8:38-39).

Let's pray.

The Son of God to Find

Adoration of the Shepherds, Matthias Stomer, 1632

The shepherds at those tidings

Rejoicèd much in mind

And left their flocks a-feeding

In tempest, storm, and wind,

And went to Bethlehem straightway

The Son of God to find,

> O tidings of comfort and joy,

> Comfort and joy,

> O tidings of comfort and joy!

The angels had more to say to the shepherds, and when the message was delivered and the Lord glorified in heavenly praise, the shepherds were left with a quiet night but very energized hearts!

"'Let us now go into Bethlehem and see this thing that has come to pass, which the Lord has made known to us.' And they came with haste ..." (Luke 2:15-16)

The song says correctly, they left their flocks to go "straightway" to the town. When King David was a young man and went to take supplies to his brothers in the army, his older brother upbraided him. *"Why did you come down here? And with whom have you left those few sheep in the wilderness?"* David answered, *"Is there not a cause?"* (1 Samuel 17:28-29) These shepherds could certainly say, "We're looking for the Son of God, and that should be cause enough for anybody."

What did they expect to find? The angels told them that the Baby would be *"wrapped in swaddling cloths, and lying in a manger"* (Luke 2:12). Surely, they knew that no ordinary infant prince would be sleeping in a stable. But then again, no ordinary prince would have choirs of angels lighting the skies. When the announcement was surrounded by the glory of God (Luke 2:9), maybe the decorations of human pride suddenly didn't seem important.

Today's painting illustrates the adoration of the shepherds when they found that child they'd been told about. Notice the way the artist uses light in their faces to show the glory of God and their faces and mannerisms to show their emotions.

The Bible doesn't tell us the weather on that fateful night. The song speaks of "tempest, storm, and wind," but that may be the poetic imagination in play. It would suggest a note of urgency in the shepherds' departure – and that much we know is true!

That may be a small reminder to us to remember, our source of Biblical truth is the Bible itself. Many illustrations or interpretations can be helpful, and sometimes telling the stories allows us to fill in gaps with sanctified imagination. Sometimes the song writer or poet may have an excellent turn of phrase – but we should always be humble, and open to a better understanding of the inspired Word of God!

Let's pray!

This Holy Tide of Christmas

Children by the Christmas tree, Leopold Kalckreuth, Before 1926

Now to the Lord sing praises,
All you within this place,
And with true love and brotherhood
Each other now embrace,
This holy tide of Christmas
All others doth deface,

O tidings of comfort and joy,

Comfort and joy,

O tidings of comfort and joy!

Folksongs persist because they are remembered and sung by real people, in everyday situations. This song is no different. While we may sing it in church, in a worship situation and formal surroundings – and there's no reason not to do that – this song is very comfortable in social gatherings and public spaces.

This last verse moves from a retelling of the gospel account to a call to worship in the present day. "To the Lord sing praises, all you within this place" is a very Biblical thought. Several of the Psalms begin with similar invitations: "Make a joyful shout to the Lord, all you lands!" (Psalm 100:1) "Clap your hands, all you peoples! Shout to God with a voice of triumph!" (Psalm 47:1) "Oh come, let us sing to the Lord! Let us shout joyfully to the Rock of our salvation." (Psalm 95:1) "Praise the Lord! For it is good to sing praises to our God," (Psalm 147:1)

But our love for God should spill over into human relationships. "By this all will know that you are My disciples, if you have love for one another," Jesus said (John 13:35). "And this commandment we have from Him: that he who loves God must love his brother also" (1 John 4:21). Paul told the church in Rome, "Be kindly affectionate to one another with brotherly love, in honor giving preference to one another," (Romans 12:10)

The last statement in this verse is a little peculiar. You may have heard of "Christmastide"; in the historical church calendar, it's the time from Christmas Day to January 5, Epiphany (when we remember the coming of the Wise Men), otherwise known as "The Twelve Days of Christmas." (Did you know that was a religious observance?) "The Tide of Christmas" is just a way of rewording it.

What could this last phrase mean – "this holy tide of Christmas / all others doth deface"? Here is one of the odd things which happen as languages change and adapt. In nearly every modern use, "deface" means to spoil or damage something. One of the old definitions of this word, though – dating back to the

1600s or so, according to the Oxford English Dictionary – is "to outshine by contrast, or to cast into the shade." So, the last phrase could be saying, "the tidings of Christmas surpass all others", or "The Christmas season is the best time of the year." Certainly, we would never think the birth of Jesus is more important than the resurrection of Jesus (they're both necessary to God's redemptive plan), so we prefer to think this phrase is just rejoicing over the celebration itself!

Many a Merry Christmas

We often sing "God Rest You Merry, Gentlemen," in our caroling parties and gatherings with family and friends. Outside of a formal worship setting, we like to conclude with the final blessing of the last verse at the end:

God bless the ruler of this house,
And send him long to reign,
And many a merry Christmas
May live to see again,
Among your friends and kindred
That live both far and near –
That God send you a happy new year,
Happy new year,
And God send you a happy new year!

This would be our prayer for you and your family as well: May you experience the blessing of God in your home and your relationships, and may He send you a healthy, happy, and productive new year – for your good and His own glory!

As we finish our advent study, this Christmas we hope you will remember and remind others that this celebration is not about us; it's about Jesus.

The gifts are a picture that God gave us the greatest gift of all.

The evergreens remind us that we have eternal life through Christ.

The red ribbons point to the blood that was shed for our sins.

The round wreaths have no beginning and no end, like our eternal God.

The gold ribbons and decorations remind us that this is the birth of a king.

The feast is a dim picture of that great feast we'll share in heaven – the Marriage Supper of the Lamb.

We have so much to rejoice about. May your Christmas be full of joy and love.

Merry Christmas!

Acknowledgments

The cover art is from an original painting by our daughter, Susannah Young. It depicts Nuremberg, Germany's ChristKindlesMarkt, one of the oldest and most famous seasonal Christmas markets in the world. It's been held since the mid-16th century with written evidence from 1628. According to a list of participants, by 1737 almost all the craftsmen in Nuremberg, 140 people, were exhibiting at the market. We believe Susannah's painting captures the incandescent beauty of the Christmas season.

We'd also like to thank all of our children, mostly grown now, John Calvin, Caleb, Matthew, Samuel, Seth, David, Susannah, and Katie. They were our test subjects years ago as we figured out how to pass on our love for hymns and explain the theology behind them. Now they are our best friends and closest confidants. Their encouragement, prayers, and advice are invaluable to us.

More Resources

Dear Friends,

We hope you've enjoyed using Christ-Centered Advent with your family! We have other resources that we hope you'll find helpful in making biblical family life practical in your home.

At RaisingRealMen.com find:

> Award-winning books on parenting and family life, like Raising Real Men, No Longer Little (for parents of tweens/preteens), and Love, Honor, and Virtue (for teen boys).

> Character-building audiobooks the whole family will enjoy.

> Gifts and adventure gear your kids will love to receive and you can feel happy about buying.

> Educational resources, help for struggling and gifted learners.

Check out Craftsman Crate – the subscription box that builds your skills – for complete kits, real tools, and artisanal craft skills you can use the rest of your life.

Listen to our podcast, Making Biblical Family Life Practical, at HalandMelanie.com/radio or wherever you listen to podcasts.

Find out about inviting us to speak at HalandMelanie.com.

May the Lord bless you as you raise your children in the faith!

Your friends,

Hal & Melanie

Made in the USA
Columbia, SC
03 December 2024

4712541OR00038